TO:

I THINK YOU ARE QUITE FUNNY
BUT THIS BOOK WILL MAKE
YOU EVEN FUNNIER.

FROM:

HILARIOUS JOKES FOR BRILLIANT BLOKES

The Classic Dad Joke & Cheesy One-liner Collection

POP PRESS

Welcome to THE essential joke handbook.

Don't be caught short without something funny to say, ever again.

Always find a perfect pick-me-up in these pages – there is at least one laugh for every day of the year here.

Whatever life throws at you, turn to this book and you'll always be on the funny side of the street.

What happened to the woman who stole a calendar on New Year's Eve?

She got 12 months.

What did the little champagne bottle call his father?

Pop!

Dracula passed out at midnight on New Year's Eve. There was a count down.

An iPhone and a firework were arrested on New Year's Eve. One was charged and the other was let off.

What do you call fifty penguins in the Arctic?

Lost. (Penguins live in Antarctica.)

Why don't polar bears eat penguins?

They can't get the wrapper off.

Knock! Knock!

Who's there?

Howard.

Howard who?

Howard you like to stand out in the cold while some idiot keeps asking 'Who's there?'

I'm scared of lifts.
So I take steps to
avoid them.

What did the detective
in the Arctic say to
the suspect?

'Where were you on
the night of September
to March?'

Why was the marine biologist sacked?

He made a mistake on porpoise.

I entered a contest for the most prominent veins. I didn't win, but I came varicose.

A bus load of tourists arrives at Runnymede. They gather around the guide who says, 'This is the spot where the barons forced King John to sign the Magna Carta.'

A fellow at the front of the crowd asks, 'When did that happen?'

'1215,' answers the guide.

The man looks at his watch and says, 'Damn! Just missed it by half an hour!'

A patient complained to his doctor, 'I've been to three other doctors and none of them agreed with your diagnosis.'

The doctor calmly replied, 'Just wait until the autopsy, then they'll see that I was right.'

What happens when a frog's car breaks down?

It gets toad.

What do we want? Low-flying plane noises! When do we want them?

NNNNNEEEEEEE-OOOOOOOOOOO-WWWWWW!

Someone stole my mood ring. I don't know how I feel about that.

What do you call a man with a crisp packet on his head?

Russell

What do you call a man with a seagull on his head?

Cliff

What do you call a man with a map on his head?

Miles

What do call a man with a coat on his head?

Mac

What do you call a man with a toilet on his head?

Lou

What do you call a woman with two toilets on her head?

Lulu

What do you call birds who stick together?

Vel-crows.

What happened to the electrician when he made a mistake?

He was grounded.

A man is talking to his friend, an economist. He says, 'I'm a walking economy.'

The friend asks, 'How so?'

'My hairline is in recession, my stomach is a victim of inflation and both of these together are putting me into a deep depression!'

Soldiers in plays like to Shakespeares.

Two wrongs don't make a right, but two Wrights can make an aeroplane.

What do you call a UFO with faulty air conditioning?

A frying saucer.

Did you hear about the red ship that crashed into the purple ship?

100 sailors were marooned.

**What do you get if
you cross an artist
with a kebab?**

Doner-tello.

**I've just seen some scones
doing the two-step.**

Were there a lot of them?

An a-bun-dance.

What do you call a line
of men waiting to
get haircuts?

A barberqueue.

I went to the still-life
exhibition. It was quite
good, but not moving.

What did the chef give to his wife on Valentine's Day?

A hug and a quiche.

What is the most romantic fruit salad?

A date with a peach.

The skeleton went to a restaurant on his own on Valentine's day. 'Table for one?' the waiter asked.

'Yes,' he replied.
'I ain't got no body.'

Who is the best person to date on a football team?

The goalie. He's a
real keeper.

Did you hear about the young couple who decided to live in a tree house?

It went well until they had a falling out.

What did the cantaloupe say to her boyfriend on Valentine's Day?

'You're one in a melon!'

What do squirrels give each other for Valentine's Day?

Forget-me-nuts.

I used to run a dating service for chickens. But I was struggling to make hens meet.

**What did one pickle
say to the other?**

You mean a great
dill to me.

**I found a wooden shoe
in my toilet today.
It was clogged.**

To whoever stole my copy of Microsoft Office, I will find you. You have my Word.

A diamond is just a lump of coal that performed well under pressure.

LAZY WISDOM . . .

I don't like the word 'lazy'. I call it 'selective participation'.

I'm doing an escape room today. Well, actually it's work, but I'm pretty sure I can get out of it.

I've realised I need to seek professional help. From a PA, a chef and a housekeeper, ideally.

**Don't half-ass anything.
Whatever you do,
use your full ass.**

**Do anything well and you
risk someone asking
you to do it again.**

**It's useful to organise
tasks into categories:
things I won't do now,
things I won't do
later and things I'll get
someone else to do.**

**What do you call a
magician who has
lost their magic?**

Ian.

**What do you call a
beehive without an exit?**

Un-bee-leave-able.

How many narcissists does it take to unscrew a lightbulb?

Just one. He simply holds onto it and the world revolves around him.

I hate Russian dolls. They're so full of themselves.

A grasshopper walks into a cocktail bar. The barman says, 'Oh wow! Did you know there's a cocktail named after you?'

'Really?' replies the grasshopper, surprised. 'There's a drink called David?'

A barman walks into a stable. 'Hello,' says the horse. 'Why the short face?'

I bought the newlyweds
an elephant for their room.

They said, 'Thank you.'

I said, 'Don't mention it.'

When the moon hits
your knees and you
mispronounce trees . . .

. . . Sycamore.

What's the leading cause of dry skin?

Towels.

I went to a wedding where two satellite dishes got married. The ceremony wasn't great but the reception was amazing.

I just found out I'm colourblind. The news came completely out of the purple!

What is the most surprising part about the story of Easter?

That a man in his thirties would have 12 friends.

How do rabbits like their beer?

Hoppy!

What can you make from a zen egg?

An ommmmmmlet.

What do you get when you cross a rabbit with shellfish?

An oyster bunny!

Why was the Easter Bunny arrested?

He was charged with hare-assment.

I was going to tell you a joke about an egg . . .

. . . but it's not all it's cracked up to be.

What make of car do shepherds drive?

Lamb drovers.

What do you call a line of rabbits jumping backwards?

A receding hare-line.

Did you hear about the man whose new garden borders caused a fence?

What kind of socks does a gardener wear?

Garden hose.

How did the graffiti artist know he was going to be caught?

The writing was on the wall.

What did the dragon say when he saw St George?

Oh no! Not more tinned food!

♫♫

Two musicians are walking down the street, and one says to the other, 'Who was that piccolo I saw you with last night?'

He indignantly replies, 'That was no piccolo, that was my fife!'

Knock, knock.

Who's there?

Watts.

Watts who?

Watts for dinner?
I'm hungry.

A guitarist arrived at the rehearsal to find the bass player and the drummer fighting. 'What's going on?' he asked.

The bass player replied, 'He de-tuned one of my strings!'

'That's OK,' said the guitarist. 'You can just tune it back up again.'

'I can't,' said the bass player. 'He won't tell me which one!'

**Don't live in denial –
you'll get wet!**

**Don't try swimming in
Paris – you'll go in Seine!**

Don't mention long rivers in Russia – it's considered Volga!

It's not hard to drown in Africa – it's actually quite Zambezi!

I've realised that tofu is
overrated. It's just
a curd to me.

What happened to the
kitchen worker who didn't
drain the pasta properly?

The chef gave him a
re-straining order.

I went for a day out at the zoo but the only exhibit was a small dog. It was a shih tzu.

What do you call an overweight E.T.?

An Extra Cholesterol!

How do you catch a door?

You wait at a door stop.

Why did the cow cross the road?

To get to the udder side.

A flea jumped over the swinging doors of a saloon, drank three whiskies and jumped out again. He picked himself up from the dirt, dusted himself down and said, 'OK, who moved my dog?'

How did the computer programmer ask out her colleague?

She asked him if he wanted to go for a byte to eat.

The melon wanted to run away to get married in Vegas but it wasn't possible. He was a cantaloupe.

Of all the vegetables, potatoes make the best detectives. They keep their eyes peeled.

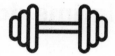

Why did the fish cross the ocean?

To get to the other tide.

How do they dance in Arabia?

Sheikh-to-sheikh.

What dance did the pilgrims do?

The Plymouth Rock.

What dance don't chickens do?

The foxtrot.

Why is it hard to get to know ballroom dancers?

They keep putting up waltz.

Where can you dance in California?

At the San Frandisco.

What sort of dance do vampires enjoy?

A fang-tango.

Why didn't the skeleton cross the road?

Because he didn't have the guts.

I'm reading a horror story in Braille. Something bad is about to happen . . . I can feel it.

What is small, red and whispers?

A hoarse radish.

How did the egg cross the road?

It scrambled across!

Two big, tough roads walk into a bar. They go to sit in their usual seat but recoil, terrified, before slinking off to sit elsewhere. The barman is surprised. Their customary table is occupied by a small, unassuming lane. Why didn't they just tell him to move, he asks the big roads.

'Haven't you heard?' they whispered in awe. 'He's a cyclepath!'

The sandwich kept
making wordplay jokes.
It was a punini.

The disorganised man
was quickly fired from his
job on the railway. He
found it too hard to keep
track of everything.

What's a soldier's favourite date?

March forth!

Did you hear about the soldier who survived mustard gas and pepper spray attacks?

He's now a seasoned veteran!

Why did the soldier stuff himself with pudding?

He was a desserter.

Where did Genghis Khan keep his armies?

Up his sleevies.

What falls, but never needs a bandage?

The rain.

Did you hear about the redundant shepherd?

He felt ewes less.

Why do engineers enjoy fixing steelwork together?

Because it's riveting.

A man just assaulted me with milk, cream and butter. How dairy.

I just broke up with my mathematician girlfriend. She was obsessed with an X.

I can't take my dog to the pond anymore because the ducks keep attacking him. That's what I get for buying a pure bread dog.

What's a lawyer's favourite drink?

Subpoena colada.

I hate it when people say age is only a number. Age is clearly a word.

Two fortune tellers met outside one of their tents on a sunny summer day. 'Lovely weather,' said the first fortune teller.

'Yes,' said the second. 'It reminds me of the summer of 2029.'

It's true that an apple a day does keep the doctor away. You just have to throw it really hard.

Did you hear about the standoff at the campground?

It was very tense.

The bowls club are going to relay their grass.

It was a turf decision.

How do you become a good gardener?

You have to know the ground rules.

A friend told me he'd dug a hole in my backyard and filled it with water. I thought he meant well.

**What's red and sits
in the corner?**

A naughty strawberry.

**Which superhero uses
public transport?**

Bus Lightyear.

Knock, knock.

Who's there?

Annie.

Annie who?

Annie more jokes? I'm running low here.

Knock, knock.

Who's there?

Inspector.

Inspector who?

Hey, I'm the one asking
the questions here.

When I bought some fruit trees, the nursery owner threw in some insects to help with pollination. They were free bees.

I'm not a fan of spring cleaning.

Let's be honest, I'm not into summer, autumn, or winter cleaning either.

What is the gooey red stuff between an elephant's toes?

Slow clowns.

A sign at a nudist camp: 'Clothed till May.'

I wanted to join my local rambling club, but the man I spoke to on the phone just went on and on.

Did you hear about these new reversible jackets? I'm excited to see how they turn out.

A band on a cruise ship was consistently bad at staying in time. Finally, the entertainment manager said, 'Either you improve or I'll throw you overboard . . . It's up to you: sync or swim.'

My colleague can no longer attend next week's Innuendo Seminar so I have to fill her slot instead.

Why are dentists sad?

Because they always look down in the mouth.

As I get older, I think more about all the people I lost along the way. Maybe becoming a tour guide was not the right choice.

Why don't schools teach astronomy?

They don't have the space.

I lost my job at the bank on my very first day. A woman asked me to check her balance, so I pushed her over.

I was addicted to
the hokey cokey but I
turned myself around.

Why do you never see
elephants hiding in trees?

Because they are very
good at it.

The past, the present, and the future walked into a bar. It was tense.

When does a joke become a dad joke?

When it becomes apparent.

I make apocalypse puns
like there's no tomorrow.

Why couldn't the sesame
seed leave the casino?

Because he was on a roll.

Why did the man sell his vacuum cleaner?

Well, it was just gathering dust.

I like elephants.

Everything else is irrelephant.

What do you call a deer with no eyes?

No eye deer.

What do you call a deer with no eyes and no legs?

A still no eye deer.

Two wind turbines are standing on the side of a hill. One asks, 'What's your favourite kind of music?'

The other says, 'I'm a big metal fan.'

What do you call a Frenchman in sandals?

Phillipe Floppe.

Two guys walk into a bar.

The third guy ducks.

Have you heard the
rumour about butter?

Never mind, I shouldn't
be spreading it.

Why shouldn't you fart in a lift?

It's wrong on a number of levels.

RIP, boiled water. You will be mist.

Passer-by: That's a pretty good ceiling.

Michelangelo: Thanks. It might not be the best but it's up there.

What's the difference between a hippo and a Zippo?

One is really heavy and the other is a little lighter.

The only thing flat
earthers have to fear . . .
is sphere itself.

What do you call a
crocodile that is also
a detective?

An investi-gator.

What do you call spaghetti pretending to be noodles?

An impasta.

What did the buffalo say when his son left?

Bison!

Policeman: We've just caught your dogs, sir. They were chasing people on bikes.

Man: That's ridiculous, officer. My dogs don't even own bikes.

What did the Zen Buddhist say to the hot dog seller?

Make me one with everything.

**What did the artist say
to the dentist?**

Matisse hurt.

**Why wouldn't the
artist's car start?**

He forgot to put in Degas.

Why was the art dealer in debt?

He didn't have any Monet.

Did you hear about the Lautrec painting that fell down in the gallery?

It was Toulouse.

**I don't trust stairs.
They're always up to
something.**

**They were a fastidious
couple.**

She was fast,
he was tedious.

Father: Son, how are your exam results?

Son: Well, Dad, they are a lot like Holland, Mauritius and the Dead Sea.

Father: What do you mean?

Son: All at C level or below.

What's purple and screams from the top of a tower?

A damson in distress.

Why could the student of French only count to seven?

She had a huit allergy.

Why did the ugly duckling stop preening himself?

He felt a little down in the mouth.

A frog found out some of his ancestors came from Warsaw.

It turned out he was a tad Polish.

What did the dirt say to the rain?

If you keep this up, my name will be mud!

Why did the gangster start dealing Filofaxes?

He was involved in organised crime.

What's the best kind of pain?

Champagne.

Buttercup and Daisy were chatting as they chewed the cud. "Ere, have you heard about this mad cow disease?'

'Yes, sounds nasty. I'm glad I'm a hippo.'

Knock, knock.

Who's there?

Europe.

Europe who?

No, you're a poo.

Knock, knock.

Who's there?

Honeydew.

Honeydew who?

Honeydew you wanna dance?

I accidentally ate someone else's Turkish takeaway and I falafel about it.

The human cannonball retired but unfortunately the position went unfilled. They couldn't find a replacement of the right calibre.

No one ever wants to babysit a naughty atom; they always have to keep an ion it.

A basketball player and a jockey robbed a bank. Police are searching high and low.

People who plug their computer keyboards into hi-fi systems aren't idiots. That would be stereotyping.

I should have been sad when my torch batteries died, but I was de-lighted.

**Monorail enthusiasts have
a one-track mind.**

**What's the difference
between a teacher
and a guard?**

One trains the mind, the
other minds the train.

Knock, knock.

Who's there?

Boo.

Boo who?

Awww, don't cry!

Why did the chicken cross the road?

To *bock* traffic.

Why did the fox cross the road?

She was chasing the chicken.

Why did the gum cross the road?

It was stuck to the chicken's foot.

Yesterday, I accidentally swallowed some food colouring. The doctor says I'm OK but I feel like I've dyed a little inside.

Did you hear about the man who swallowed a pillow?

His condition was described as comfortable.

Can a panda touch its toes?

Bearly.

Why did the egg hide?

It was a little chicken.

What do you call an arrogant fugitive falling from a building?

Condescending.

The chickens were distraught when the tornado destroyed their home. Hopefully they will be able to recoup.

Did you hear about the man who was caught trying to steal stamps?

He philately denied it.

What do you call a rich bear?

Winnie the pools.

What happens if you are in a love triangle?

It soon becomes a wreck-tangle.

Two people who went skating on a first date fell through a frozen pond. At least it broke the ice.

Why did the sheep cross the road?

To get to the baa-baa shop for a haircut.

Why did the turtle cross the road?

To get to the Shell station.

Why did the rooster cross the road?

He had something to cock-a-doodle dooo!

Golf is a lot like taxes — you drive hard to get to the green and end up in the hole.

Marathon runners with bad footwear suffer the agony of defeat.

Do the people who climb the world's highest mountain ever rest?

Swimming can be easy or hard. It deep-ends.

What do arrogant cheerleaders have?

Pompomposity.

What do prize fighters do before and after work?

Punch in and punch out.

Why did the rubber chicken cross the road?

To stretch her legs.

Why did the clown cross the road?

To retrieve his rubber chicken.

My dentist told me I
needed a crown. Finally,
someone realised.

My computer's got the
Miley virus. It's stopped
twerking.

When bungee-jumping,
never ask anyone to cut
you some slack.

How do tennis players
insult each other?

They give backhanded
compliments.

What do you call a group
of Olympic swimmers?

A talent pool.

What's the best diet
for a gymnast?

A balanced one.

Why is it a good idea to
employ a successful
100-metre runner?

Because they have a
good track record.

Sky have just won the
rights to screen the first
World Origami
Championships from
Tokyo. Unfortunately,
it's only available on
Paper View.

IRONIC WISDOM . . .

May your coffee be strong
and your Monday short.

Money isn't everything,
but it helps make sure the
kids stay in touch.

As you slide down the
banister of life, may the
splinters never point in the
wrong direction.

You need only two tools:
WD-40 and duct tape.
If it doesn't move and it
should, use WD-40.
If it moves and shouldn't,
use the tape.

Don't sweat the petty
things, and don't pet the
sweaty things.

I don't want to have to worry about money. Your job will be to take on all the money worries.'

'I see,' the accountant said. 'And how much does the job pay?'

'I'll start you at eighty thousand.'

'Eighty thousand pounds!' the accountant exclaimed. 'How can such a small business afford that?'

'That,' the owner said, 'is your first worry.'

When can police search
your house?

When it's warranted.

A dry cleaner was indicted
with charges pressed for
money laundering. A deal
is being ironed out.

Two robbers were robbing a hotel. The first one said, 'I hear sirens. Jump!'

The second one said, 'But we're on the thirteenth floor!'

The first one screamed back, 'This is no time to be superstitious!'

Why was the hand
arguing?

Three fingers were willing
to cooperate but the
thumb and forefinger
were opposed.

Which singer is best at
getting the lids off a
jam jars?

Kris Twistofferson.

**Fishing is very addictive.
You can really get hooked.**

**A ham discharged
himself from hospital.
He was cured.**

How many vegetarians does it take to eat a cow?

One, if nobody's looking.

Why was the dumpling arrested?

For wonton disregard of the law.

An old lady was waiting to park when a young man in his brand-new car drove around her and took the space that she had been waiting for. She was so annoyed that she approached the young fellow and said, through gritted teeth, 'I was about to park there.'

The man looked at her with disdain and replied, 'That's what you can do when you're young and fast.'

This annoyed the old lady even more, so she got back in her car, backed it up and then stamped on the accelerator, ramming straight into his car.

The young man ran back to his car and shouted in a stunned voice, 'What did you do that for?'

She smiled at him and said, 'That's what you can do when you're old and rich.'

Did you hear the Kennel Club are in financial difficulty?

They might have to call in the retrievers.

How does the Pope pay for stuff on eBay?

Papal.

Why did the strawberry cross the road?

There was a traffic jam!

What kind of snack do astronauts like?

Mars bars.

What is the best thing about living in Switzerland?

Well, the flag is a big plus.

Why is there always so much dirt on the forest floor?

Because nature abhors a vacuum.

A speeding motorist was caught by radar from a police helicopter in the sky. An officer pulled him over and began to issue a speeding ticket. 'How did you know I was speeding?' the frustrated driver asked.

The police officer pointed towards the sky.

'You mean,' asked the motorist, aghast, 'that even He is against me?'

What's the biggest city in Europe?

Dublin – it keeps Dublin and Dublin!

Did you hear about the budgie that was sacked from the pet shop?

It had its hands in the Trill.

A man walks into a bar to find a horse there serving drinks. The horse asks, 'What are you staring at? Haven't you ever seen a horse working behind a bar before?'

The guy says, 'It's not that. I just never thought the parrot would sell the place.'

Did you hear about the restaurant on the moon?

Great food, no atmosphere.

A woman told her boyfriend that she couldn't stay with him as he had no sense of direction. So he packed up his stuff and right.

I've been breeding racing deer. I'm hoping to make a quick buck.

What do you get if you cross a painter with a boxer?

Muhammad Dali.

A cheese factory exploded in France scattering da brie everywhere.

What kind of cheese can hide a horse?

Mascarpone.

What did the cheese say when it saw itself in the mirror?

Haloumi!

What kind of dinosaur is made entirely of cheese?

Gorgonzilla.

A file arrives on a secret agent's desk. On the front in red letters it says: 'TOP SECRET: JAM.' The general opens the file to see what it could be. Inside is a single piece of paper. Printed on it is: 'I can't tell you more in case you spread it about.'

The criminal mastermind found one of his gang sawing the legs off his bed. 'What are you doing that for?' demanded the boss.

'Only doing what you ordered,' said the thug. 'You told me to lie low for a bit!'

Doctor, Doctor! I think I'm turning into an orange!

Have you tried playing squash?

Doctor, Doctor! Everyone thinks I am a liar!

Well, I find that hard to believe.

Doctor, Doctor! I think I'm a curtain!

You need to pull yourself together.

**Doctor, Doctor! I think I'm
a snooker ball!**

I'm afraid you're going to
have to join the back
of the cue.

**Doctor, Doctor! I've broken
my arm in two places!**

I'd strongly advise you not
to go back to either of
those places.

**Doctor, Doctor! I've a
strawberry stuck in
my ear!**

Don't worry, I've some
cream for that.

Did you hear about the two cheerleaders who got married?

They met by chants.

I went to that new restaurant, Karma. There's no menu, you just get what you deserve.

No matter how kind you are, German children are kinder.

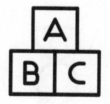

How did one witch speak to the other?

She cauldron the phone.

What do you call a
mummy covered in
chocolate and nuts?

A Pharaoh Roche.

Why do demons and
ghouls hang out together?

Because demons are a
ghoul's best friend.

**Why did the ghost
starch his sheet?**

He wanted everyone
scared stiff.

**Why don't mummies
take time off?**

They're afraid to unwind.

What's the difference between an onion and an accordion?

No one cries when you chop up an accordion.

How do you know when a banjo has been tuned?

No one knows, it's never been done.

What's the difference between a vacuum cleaner and the bagpipes?

Bagpipes don't need to be plugged in to suck.

How do you know when a drum solo's really bad?

The bass player notices.

Why are harps like elderly parents?

Both are unforgiving and hard to get into and out of cars.

Why was the piano invented?

So musicians would have a place to put their beer.

Why are witches advised not to use their brooms when angry?

In case they fly off the handle.

What's the scariest type of cutlery?

A spoooooon!

Parallel lines have so much in common. It's a shame they'll never meet.

I threw a boomerang a few years ago. I now live in constant fear.

A book just fell on my head. I've only got my shelf to blame.

Last night, I kept dreaming that I had written *Lord of the Rings*. My wife said I'd been Tolkien in my sleep.

I'm reading a book about anti-gravity. It's impossible to put down.

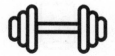

Did you hear about the high-ranking military father who cloned himself?

The result was a Major Faux Pa.

COWBOY WISDOM . . .

Never squat with spurs on.

The only good reason to ride a bull is to meet a nurse.

Always drink upstream of the herd.

Never ask how stupid
someone is because
they'll turn around and
show you.

Cowboys don't take
baths, they just dust off.

Cowboys don't volunteer
for the rodeo, they have
to be roped into it.

A man walks into a pub and sees the daily special written on the blackboard: A pie, a pint and a kind word, £3.

'That's a bargain,' he thinks to himself, 'I'll have some of that.'

Sitting down at the bar with his pint of beer in one hand and his meat pie in the other, he asks the barman, 'What's the kind word?'

Shaking his head the barman says, 'Wouldn't eat that pie if I was you.'

Did you hear about the artist who was found dead?

All the details are sketchy.

Did you know Jesus drove a Honda but didn't talk about it?

John 12:49: 'For I did not speak of my own accord.'

I support both of my wives very well. I think that's big o' me.

Why was the farmer stuffing sheep into his computer?

It needed more RAM.

'My boyfriend drives his car like lightning.'

'You mean he drives very fast?'

'No, he hits trees.'

A clown decided to retire and hand over the business to his son. His son said, 'I don't know, Dad, those are big shoes to fill.'

What do you get if you cross a sheepdog with a jelly?

The collie wobbles.

What is Dracula's favourite dog breed?

Bloodhound.

What do you get when you cross a dog with a cougar?

A lot of trouble with the postman.

What do you call a dog magician?

A Labracadabrador.

What's E.T. short for?

He's only got little legs.

What's the difference between ignorance and apathy?

I don't know and
I don't care.

Did you hear about the man arrested in the butcher's?

He was choplifting.

Why are phlebotomists good proofreaders?

Because they can spot type-O's.

What would you get if you crossed a cat and a donkey?

A mewl.

What do you call the cat that was caught by the police?

The purrpetrator.

Why can't cats play poker in the jungle?

Too many cheetahs.

What do cats eat for breakfast?

Mice Krispies!

His hair was blonde and his head was angular: he was fair and square.

Two cab drivers met. 'Hey,' asked one, 'why did you paint one side of your cab red and the other side blue?'

'Well,' the other responded, 'when I get into an accident, you should see how all the witnesses contradict each other.'

Did you hear about the astronomer who left his job to become a barber?

Eclipse hair now.

What did King Arthur listen to every evening at six?

The knightly news.

How do heart surgeons get to hospital?

They use the bypass.

What do you get if you've got an infected organ?

Bach-ache.

What do you call it when there aren't enough nurses on the delivery ward?

A midwife crisis.

Chiropodists are expensive: they charge by the foot.

The optician wanted to start his own business but worried he didn't have enough contacts.

Why should you never lie to an X-ray technician?

They can see right through you.

What happens when it rains cats and dogs?

You have to be careful not to step in a poodle.

Be kind to your dentist because she has fillings too.

A brain walks into a bar and takes a seat. 'I'd like some wings and a pint of beer, please,' it says.

'Sorry, but I can't serve you,' the bartender replies. 'You're out of your head.'

My son's fourth birthday was today. When he came to see me, I didn't recognise him at first. I had never seen him be four.

What is a pumpkin's favourite sport?

Squash.

Why do a pilgrim's pants always fall down?

Because they wear their belt buckle on their hat.

What would you get if you crossed a turkey with a ghost?

A poultrygeist!

What do you get if you divide the circumference of a pumpkin by its diameter?

Pumpkin pi.

What's the most musical part of a turkey?

The drumstick.

Did you hear about the man who was addicted to Thanksgiving leftovers?

He wanted to stop but couldn't quit cold turkey.

This girl thought she recognised me from vegetarian club, but I'd never met herbivore.

'Waiter!' shouted the furious diner. 'How dare you serve me this? There's a TWIG in my soup!'

'My apologies,' said the waiter. 'I'll inform the branch manager.'

My grief counsellor died. He was so good that I didn't even mind.

I remember the last words my grandfather told me right before he kicked the bucket. He said, 'Wanna see how far I can kick this bucket?'

Why couldn't the sunflower ride its bike?

It lost its petals.

Why did the PowerPoint presentation cross the road?

To get to the other slide.

Why did the dog cross the road twice?

He was playing fetch with a boomerang.

Why did the chicken cross the road?

Because it was free-range!

I was going to tell you a joke about boxing . . .

but I forgot the punch line.

It's possible to throw a party in space – you just have to planet.

Somebody stole all my lamps . . . I was de-lighted.

What's the best time on a clock?

6:30, hands down.

What did the grape say when it got stepped on?

Nothing, it just let out a little whine.

Doctor: 'Sir, I'm afraid your DNA is backwards.'

Patient: 'And?'

What does C.S. Lewis keep in his wardrobe?

Narnia business.

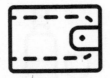

How do you stop a bull from charging?

Cancel its credit card.

What beats his chest and swings from Christmas cake to Christmas cake?

Tarzipan.

Why did the little boy call Father Christmas Santa Cause?

Because there was Noel.

What happens when you eat Christmas decorations?

You get tinsel-itus.

Will the Christmas pudding be long?

No, it'll be the traditional round.

Who is in charge of risk assessment in Santa's workshop?

The elf and safety officer.

Why are Christmas trees bad at knitting?

They drop their needles.

How does Rudolph know when Christmas is coming?

He looks at his calen-deer.

What kind of key can't open doors?

A tur-key.

What's Scrooge's favourite Christmas game?

Mean-opoly.

How does Darth Vader enjoy his Christmas Turkey?

On the dark side.

Santa Claus's elves are subordinate clauses.

How did the salt and pepper welcome all the guests?

By saying, 'Seasoning's greetings!'

It was Christmas and the judge was in a merry mood as he asked the prisoner, 'What are you charged with?'

'Doing my Christmas shopping early,' replied the defendant.

'That's no offence,' said the judge. 'How early were you doing this shopping?'

'Before the store opened,' explained the prisoner.

Pop Press, an imprint of Ebury Publishing
20 Vauxhall Bridge Road
London SW1V 2SA

Pop Press is part of the Penguin Random House group of companies
whose addresses can be found at global.penguinrandomhouse.com

Penguin
Random House
UK

First published by Pop Press in 2023

www.penguin.co.uk

A CIP catalogue record for this book is available from the British Library

ISBN 9781529927085

Typeset in 20/25pt TT Fors by Jouve (UK), Milton Keynes
Printed and bound in Great Britain by Clays Ltd, Elcograf S.p.A.

The authorised representative in the EEA is Penguin Random House
Ireland, Morrison Chambers, 32 Nassau Street, Dublin D02 YH68

Penguin Random House is committed to a sustainable future
for our business, our readers and our planet. This book is made
from Forest Stewardship Council® certified paper.

MIX
Paper | Supporting
responsible forestry
FSC® C018179